# Fun with Flowcharts

Following Instructions

Anna McDou

# COMPUTER
# SCIENCE For the REAL World™

## Rosen Classroom™

Published in 2018 by The Rosen Publishing Group, Inc.
29 East 21st Street, New York, NY 10010

Book Design: Jennifer Ryder-Talbot
Editor: Caitie McAneney

Photo Credits: Cover michaeljung/Shutterstock.com; p. 4 violetkaipa/
Shutterstock.com; p. 4-21 schab/Shutterstock.com; p. 8 ponomareva/S
hutterstock.com; p.8 (water inset) LoopAll/Shutterstock.com; p. 11 Pinkyone/
Shutterstock.com; p. 12-13 Chones/Shutterstock.com; p. 14 Evgeniia Litovchenko/
Shutterstock.com; p. 17 Phototalker/Shutterstock.com; p. 18 Monkey Business Images/
Shutterstock.com; p. 21 piotr_pabijan/Shutterstock.com.

Library of Congress Cataloging-in-Publication Data

Names: McDougal, Anna.
Title: Fun with flowcharts: following instructions / Anna McDougal.
Description: New York : Rosen Classroom, 2018. | Series: Computer Kids: Powered by
Computational Thinking | Includes glossary and index.
Identifiers: LCCN ISBN 9781508137856 (pbk.) | ISBN 9781538324011 (library bound) |
ISBN 9781538353240 (6pack) | ISBN 9781508137467 (ebook)
Subjects: LCSH: Science--Methodology--Juvenile literature. | Research--Methodology--
Juvenile literature.
Classification: LCC Q175.2 M33 2018 | DDC 507.2'1--dc23

Manufactured in the United States of America

CPSIA Compliance Information: Batch #WS18RC: For Further Information contact Rosen Publishing, New York, New York at 1-800-237-9932

# Table of Contents

Flowcharts are used in science, business, and even coding.

4

# What Is a Flowchart?

Have you ever worked on an experiment in science class? All that we know about science is thanks to experiments. People come up with a **hypothesis** and then test it to see if it's true.

Most experiments have many steps. It can be hard to keep track of all of the steps. However, you can use a flowchart. A flowchart is a diagram that shows a **progression** of steps using connecting lines. Flowcharts can help you do an experiment step by step in a way that's easy to follow.

# The Scientific Method

Scientists rely on the scientific method when they're performing experiments. The scientific method is a **process** for experiments that has been used for hundreds of years. Scientists follow this method with each experiment.

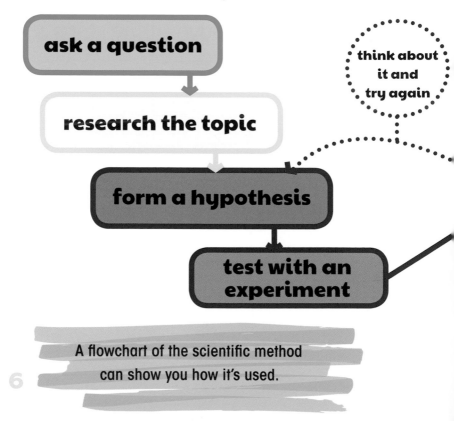

A flowchart of the scientific method can show you how it's used.

First, you need to ask a question. For example, "Will heavy and light objects fall at the same rate?" Next, you must **research** the topic and form a hypothesis. Test the hypothesis through an experiment and learn from the results. If the experiment works differently than you expected, you can change it and try again.

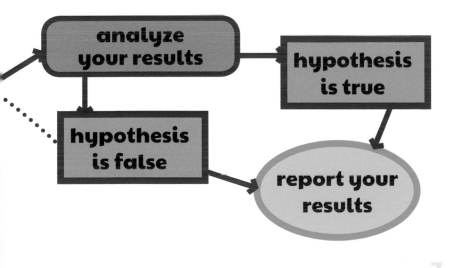

Water molecules are the smallest parts of water that are still water.

$H_2O$

# Creating an Experiment

Think of the kind of experiment you'd like to do. It all starts with a question. Will a balloon shrink in cold air? What happens when baking soda and vinegar mix? Will sugar **dissolve** in water?

Imagine that you want to make an experiment that answers this question: Do molecules move faster in hot or cold water? First, do your research. You will find that molecules are the smallest parts of a **substance** that still have all the **properties** of that substance.

# What Is the Hypothesis?

Once you ask a question and research the topic, you can make an educated guess about the answer. That's the hypothesis. You may be fairly certain about what you think will happen. It's still important to do the experiment to find out for sure.

For this experiment, your hypothesis might be "molecules move faster in hot water." This could be based on your research about how molecules act in different **conditions**. However, you might guess the opposite. There's only one way to find out!

Researching a topic gives you an idea about what your hypothesis might be.

# Test It Out

Now it's time to test your hypothesis. This part of an experiment will have its own steps.

In experiments, you want to keep some conditions the same. Have the same amount of water in each cup.

First, gather three clear cups or jars. Using masking tape and a marker, label them as cold water, room temperature water, and hot water. Fill the first cup with very cold water. Fill the second cup with room temperature water—not too warm or cold. Fill the third cup with water that you boil in the microwave or on the stove. Lastly, add a drop of food dye to each cup.

Look at the dye just after it hits
the water. How quickly does it spread?

# The Results Are In!

The food dye will start to sink into the water. Watch how it acts in each of the three cups. Does it act the same? Does it act differently?

You will notice that the food dye spreads most quickly in the hot water. The food dye should move slowly in the cold water. The room temperature water should have results in the middle. The results of this experiment support the hypothesis that molecules move faster in hot water.

# Try Again

What happens if your hypothesis was wrong? Maybe you guessed that molecules moved faster in cold water. In that case, you can go back and adjust your hypothesis with the information you know now.

If any part of an experiment doesn't go the way it's supposed to, you can go back and try it again. Sometimes scientists try an experiment with new **variables**. This can further support their hypothesis. A key to adding new variables is to test them one at a time.

If you change your experiment, be sure to fix your flowchart to show the change.

What's your **conclusion?**
You can present your
results to your class.

# Reporting Results

The last step in an experiment is to report your results. Through your experiment results, you should have come to a conclusion. What did the experiment tell you? What do you believe to be true?

You can report your results to teach others about molecules. Make a statement, such as: "The food dye moved most quickly in hot water, which leads to the conclusion that molecules move faster in hot water." People might use the results of your experiment when they research a topic for their own experiment!

# Making a Flowchart

Making an experiment flowchart can help people understand your results or recreate the experiment. The flowchart should break the experiment down into small, easy tasks.

Start with the first step, such as "gather materials." Then, draw an arrow to the next step—"label cups." Sometimes, the flowchart might break into two arrows. You might write "if yes, then" and "if no, then" and connect those phrases to arrows. In this case, the next step will depend on the results of the previous step.

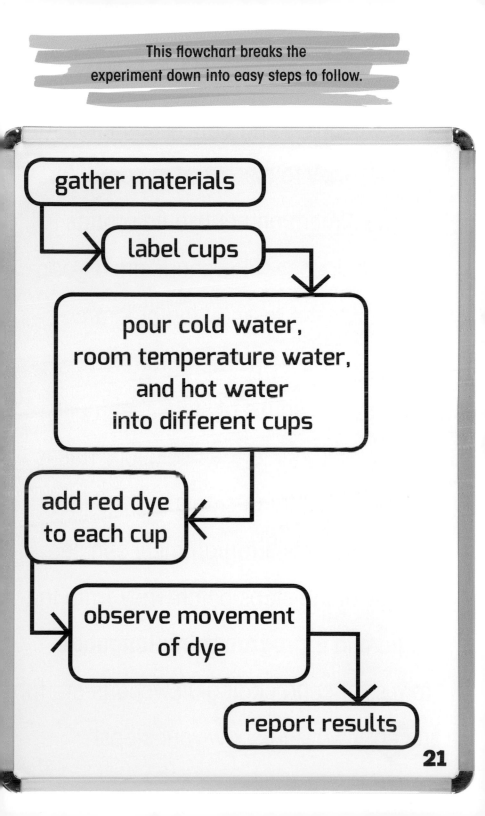

gather materials

label cups

pour cold water,
room temperature water,
and hot water
into different cups

add red dye
to each cup

observe movement
of dye

report results

# Flowcharts in Coding

Flowcharts aren't only used in natural science. They're also used in computer science. Programmers use flowcharts to create their code. Flowcharts are a good way to plan the tasks of the program.

A flowchart helps a programmer **illustrate** the series of steps that must be performed to get to their solution. This is especially helpful in creating a program with many parts. Programmers can see the flow of the steps before they write the program in a **programming language**. From science to coding, flowcharts are fun and easy ways to show your steps!

# Glossary

**conclusion:** A judgment based on reason.

**condition:** A state of being.

**dissolve:** To mix completely into a liquid.

**hypothesis:** An educated guess.

**illustrate:** To show something in a picture.

**process:** A set of steps.

**programming language:** A language that gives directions to a machine, especially a computer.

**progression:** Moving forward from one step to another.

**property:** A quality or trait belonging to something.

**research:** Studying to find something new.

**substance:** Matter with a specific chemical makeup.

**variable:** A quantity that may change when other conditions change.

# Index